IF YOU LOVE READING, THANK

JOHANNES GUTENBERG!

BIOGRAPHY 3RD GRADE

Children's Biography Books

Speedy Publishing LLC
40 E. Main St. #1156
Newark, DE 19711
www.speedypublishing.com

In this book, we're going to talk about the life of Johannes Gutenberg. So, let's get right to it!

Johannes Gutenberg

WHO WAS JOHANNES GUTENBERG?

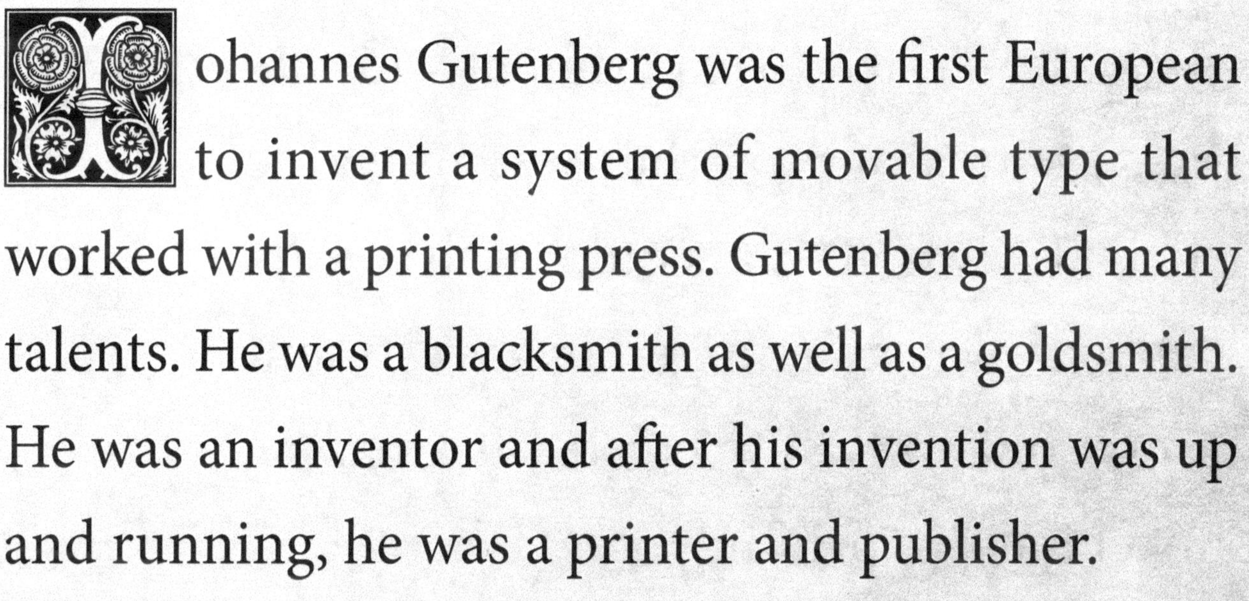

ohannes Gutenberg was the first European to invent a system of movable type that worked with a printing press. Gutenberg had many talents. He was a blacksmith as well as a goldsmith. He was an inventor and after his invention was up and running, he was a printer and publisher.

He started to experiment with the idea of type that was movable when he was 40 years old. Twelve years later he was able to get an investment from Johann Fust to create his amazing machine, the printing press.

Et la lumiere
fut

Early Life

Gutenberg was born in 1398 in the city of Mainz, Germany. His father was a goldsmith. Little is known about his childhood except that his family moved around the country a few times. While living in Mainz, Gutenberg learned his father's trade. In 1428, many craftsmen were sent into exile from the city, including Gutenberg's family.

Illustration of Johannes Gutenberg.

The reason was there had been a rebellion against the wealthy class who were ruling the town. Gutenberg fled to Strasbourg in France where he stayed until 1444.

While living in Strasbourg, Gutenberg began to work on some printing experiments. Up until this time, printing was done with wooden blocks. Gutenberg was well versed in making books already, so he understood the steps involved in making a finished book. He began to make the process of typesetting more flexible.

Johannes Gutenberg.

ABCD
EFGH
IKLM

Johannes Gutenberg Memorial Statue.

is first innovation was movable metal type. He made single letters and characters out of small metal pieces that could be moved and rearranged in different ways. Although a system of movable type with ceramic porcelain pieces had been used in China for centuries, Gutenberg's casting system and the use of alloys of metal made the creation of the type much easier. He also created oil-based inks.

utenberg took existing methods for different types of presses and adapted them to make a machine that could work with his movable type. When he operated his press, he could print thousands of pages per day instead of the standard 40 or so pages per day that was possible with wood block printing. His new machine started a reading revolution.

Printing compositors stick and type case.

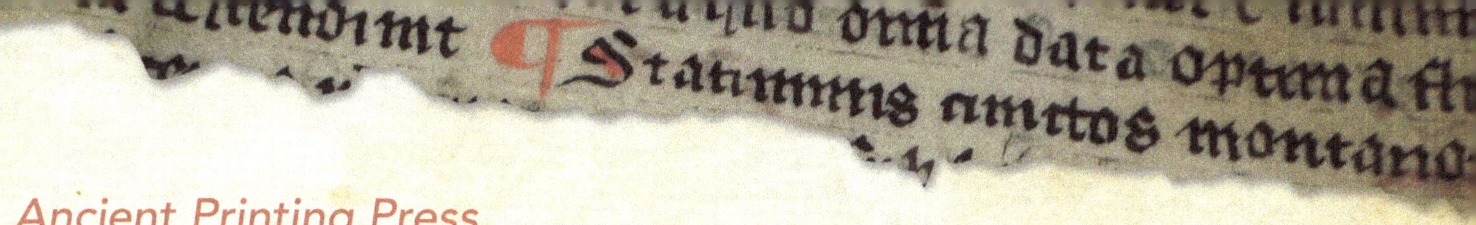

Ancient Printing Press.

Prior to this time, only wealthy people owned books because they were so expensive to produce. As the cost of printing books decreased, middle class people could afford them. Gutenberg's machine became popular across Europe very quickly. Books were printed at a pace they had never been created before.

n addition to religious books, such as the Bible, soon there was a need for travel books. By reading, people could travel to distant lands and learn about the world without even leaving their homes. The change in knowledge, education, and literacy was rapid and the world was transformed forever. Many people started to learn to read and to enjoy reading as a pastime as well as for studying.

William Caxton showing specimens of his printing to
King Edward IV and his Queen.

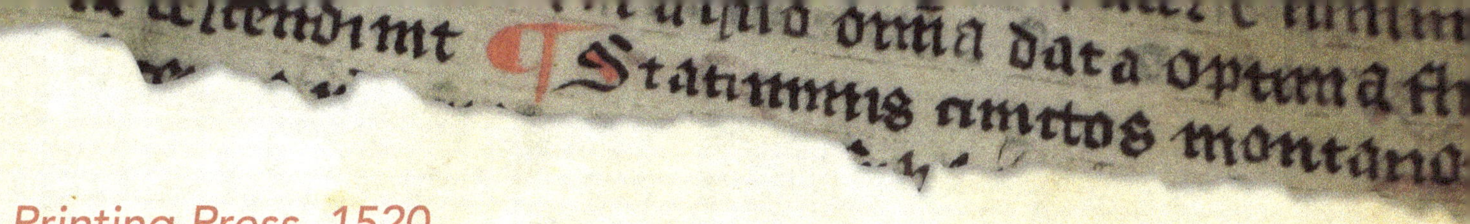

Printing Press, 1520.

There was a chance for the ordinary person to obtain knowledge through the wonders of reading. It was as if someone had turned a light on in a dark room. Gutenberg's invention had started a transformation in society that eventually helped bring about the Scientific Revolution as well as the blossoming of art and culture during the High Renaissance period.

Printing Press Tools

Deus of
Texas

Which Were The First Books Printed By Gutenberg?

Historians believe that the first printed sheet from the Gutenberg press was a poem written in German. Other printed materials were books for learning Latin grammar as well as indulgences used by the Catholic Church. These indulgences were issued to people so they wouldn't spend too much time in purgatory after they died.

The Gutenberg Bible.

However, Gutenberg's masterpiece was his Bible. It was the first time that a Bible had been produced by machine. They had always been painstakingly transcribed by hand. For the first time, the Bible was available to individuals who were not clergymen. Prior to Gutenberg's time, Bibles were very rare. It might take a monk an entire year to transcribe a Bible by hand.

Ancient Texts.

The **_Gutenberg Bible_** was written in Latin and had two columns on most pages with 42 lines of type. Most of the Bibles he created had 1,286 pages. They were so big that they had to be bound in two different volumes. Gutenberg only printed 180 of these Bibles, but they were amazing books. Only 49 copies have survived to today and many of them have missing pages.

Gutenberg Bible (Pelplin copy).

Incipit prologus sancti iheronimi
presbiteri in parabolas salomonis.
Iungat epistola quos iungit sacerdoti-
um: immo carta non diuidat: quos
xpi nectit amor. Comentarios in ose-
amos. z zachariam malachiam quoq;
poscitis. Scripsissem si licuisset pre vali-
tudine. Mittitis solacia sumptuum
notarios nostros et librarios sustenta-
tis: ut vobis potissimum nostrum desudet
ingenium. Et ecce ex latere frequens turba
diuersa poscentium: quasi aut equum sit me
vobis esurientibus aliis laborare: aut
in ratione dati et accepti cuiquam preter
vos obnoxius sim. Itaq; longa egrota-
tione fractus: ne penitus hoc anno re-
ticerem. z apud vos mutus essem: tridui
opus nomini vestro consecraui: interp-
tatione videlicet trium salomonis vo-
luminum: masloth quod hebrei parabolas:
vulgata editio prouerbia vocat: coeleth
quem grece ecclesiasten latine cocionatorem
possumus dicere: sirasirim. quod in lingua
nostram vertice canticum canticorum. Fertur et
panaretos. ihesu filij sirach liber: z alius
pseudographus. qui sapientia salomonis inscribit. Quorum priore hebra-
icum reperi. non ecclesiasticum ut apud la-
tinos: sed parabolas prenotatum. Cui iuncti
erant ecclesiastes. et canticum canticorum: ut
similitudinem salomonis. non solum nu-
mero librorum: sed etiam materiae gene-
re coequaret. Secundus apud hebreos
nusquam est: quia et ipse stilus grecam
eloquentiam redolet: et nonnulli scriptorum
veterum hunc esse iudei filonis affirmant.
Sicut ergo iudith z thobie z macha-
beorum libros: legit quidem eos ecclesia. sed
inter canonicas scripturas non recipit:
sic z hec duo volumina legat ad edi-
ficationem plebis: non ad auctoritatem
ecclesiasticorum dogmatum confirmandam.

Si qui sane septuaginta interpretum
magis editio placet: habet eam a nobis
olim emendatam. Atq; eni noua sic cu-
dimus: ut vetera destruamus. Et tamen cum
diligentissime legerit: sciat magis nostra
scripta intelligi: que non in tertium vas
transfusa coacuerit: sed statim de prelo
purissime emendata teste: suum saporem ser-
uauerit. Incipiunt parabole salomonis.

Parabole salomonis
filij dauid regis israel:
ad sciendam sapienti-
am z disciplinam: ad
intelligenda verba
prudentie et suscipi-
enda eruditione doctrine: iustitiam
et iudicium z equitatem: ut detur paruulis
astutia: et adolescenti scientia z intel-
lectus. Audiens sapiens sapientior erit: z
intelligens gubernacula possidebit. Ani-
maduertet parabolam et interpretatio-
nem: verba sapientium z enigmata eorum.
Timor domini principium sapientie. Sapien-
tiam atq; doctrinam stulti despiciunt.
Audi fili mi disciplinam patris tui et ne
dimittas legem matris tue: ut addatur
gratia capiti tuo: z torques collo tuo.
Fili mi si te lactauerint peccatores: ne ac-
quiescas eis. Si dixerint veni nobiscum
insidiemur sanguini: abscondam insi-
dias contra insontem frustra: degluti-
amus eum sicut infernus viuentem z inte-
grum: quasi descendentem in lacum: omnem
preciosam substantiam reperiemus: implebimus
domos nostras spoliis: sortem mitte nobiscum: marsupium sit unum omnium
nostrum: fili mi ne ambules cum eis. Prohi-
be pedem tuum a semitis eorum. Pedes
enim illorum ad malum currunt: z festinant ut
effundant sanguinem. Frustra autem
iacitur rete ante oculos pennatorum. Ipsi quoq;
contra sanguinem suum insidiantur: et

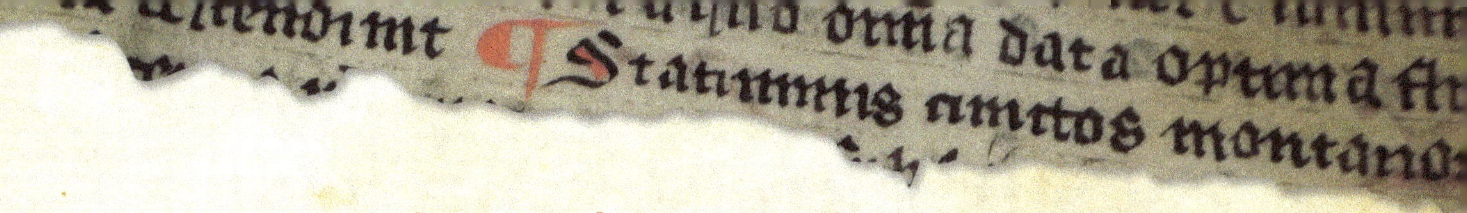

It's estimated that if a complete copy were to be auctioned today it would be purchased for $35 million dollars or more. Unfortunately, despite the fact that in his day the Bibles were each sold for a large sum, 30 gold coins named florins, Gutenberg never made much money from his work.

Gutenberg's Financial Troubles

Gutenberg invented the printing press in 1444 AD. In 1448, he left Strasbourg and returned to Mainz. Two years later he had set up his own print shop. He had borrowed a large amount of money from an investor by the name of Johann Fust so he could set up his business. Gutenberg needed the money to create his unique movable type and printing presses.

Johann Fust (1400-1466).

Printer in 1568.

By 1452 Gutenberg was in debt and he couldn't pay Fust back. A new agreement was put into place so that Fust would be a full partner in Gutenberg's printing business.

Peter Schoeffer, who was Fust's son-in-law, joined the project and historians believe that he and Gutenberg set up two presses to print the 42-line Gutenberg Bible. Schoeffer became Gutenberg's apprentice. It's believed that Schoeffer created some of the first typefaces, which are different styles and designs of type.

ſtendunt ⁋ Statuimus amictos montáno

data optíma fri

Gutenberg Bible.

In 1455, the business was making money from the indulgences the Church was having printed and also from the Bibles, but Gutenberg was still in debt. Fust had invested 1,600 florins in the business and the debt was now a huge 20,000 florins. Fust sued Gutenberg and Gutenberg lost the lawsuit. Fust now gained control over the print shop and half of Gutenberg's beautifully printed Bibles belonged to Fust.

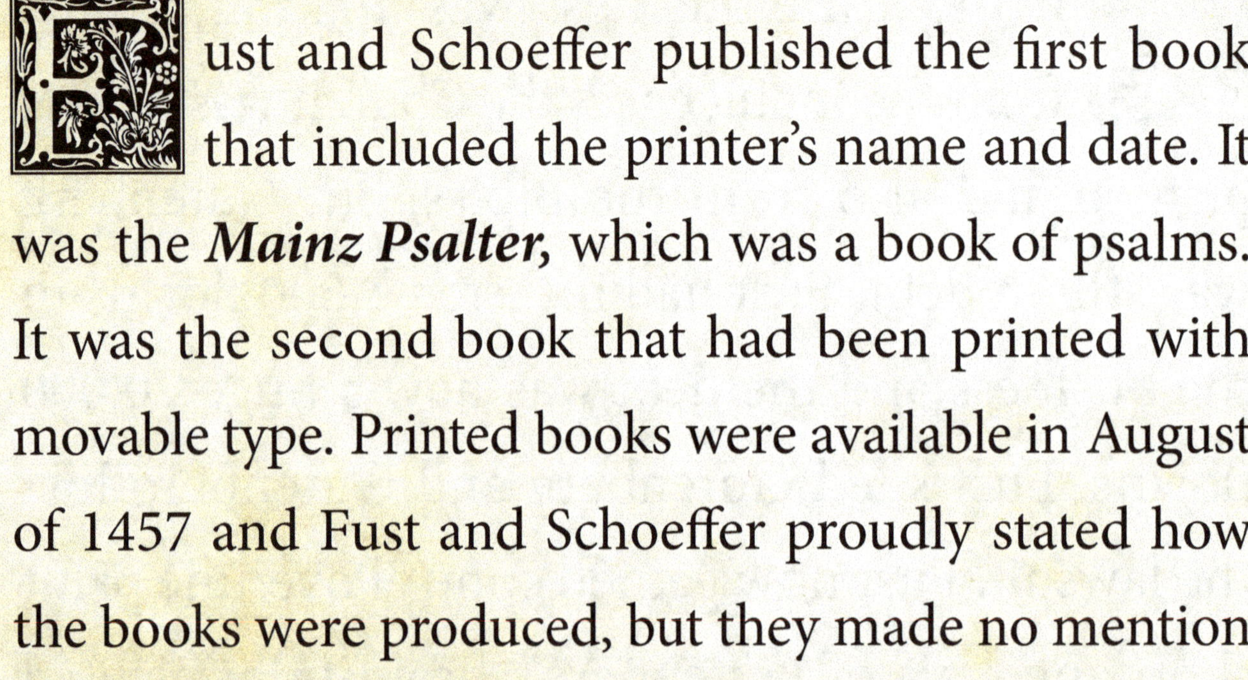

Fust and Schoeffer published the first book that included the printer's name and date. It was the *Mainz Psalter,* which was a book of psalms. It was the second book that had been printed with movable type. Printed books were available in August of 1457 and Fust and Schoeffer proudly stated how the books were produced, but they made no mention of the inventor of their presses—Gutenberg.

Mainz Psalter: Johann Fust & Peter Schoeffer (printers).

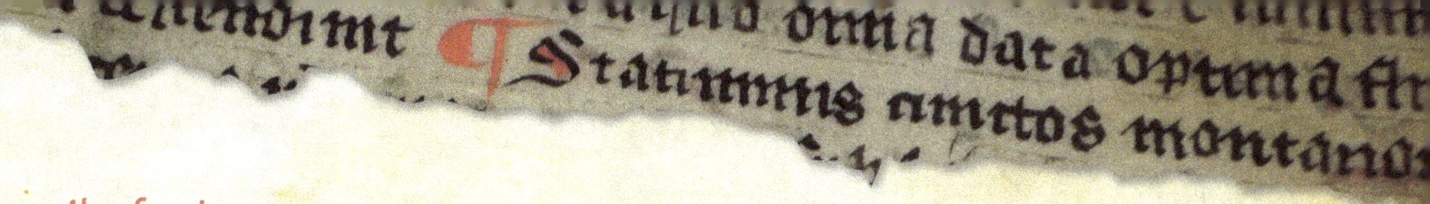

Detail of a Letterpress.

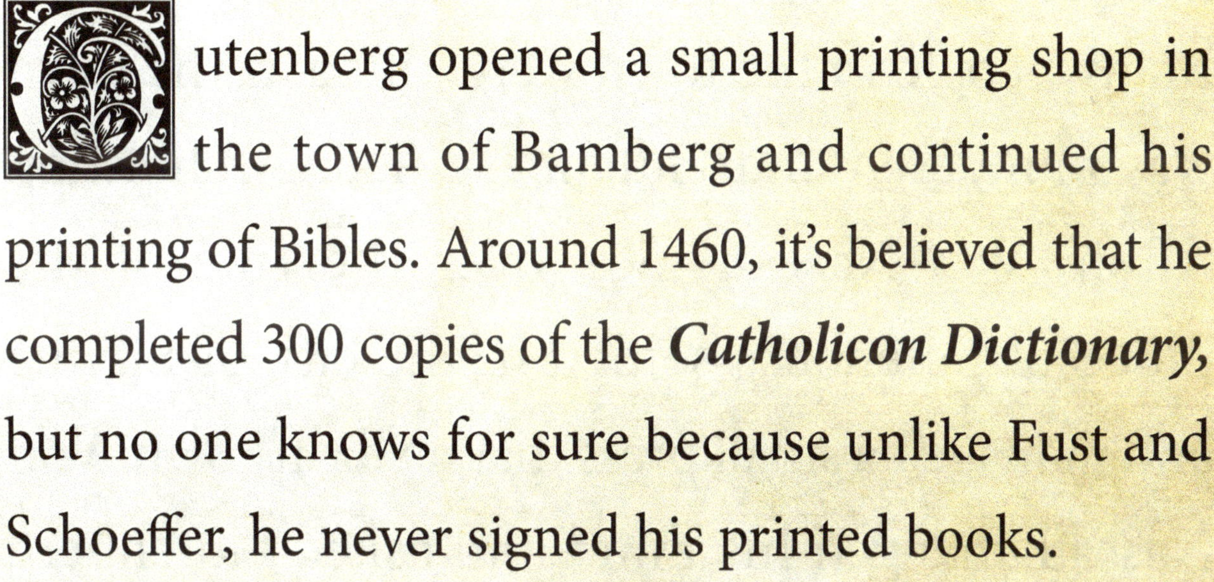

Gutenberg opened a small printing shop in the town of Bamberg and continued his printing of Bibles. Around 1460, it's believed that he completed 300 copies of the *Catholicon Dictionary,* but no one knows for sure because unlike Fust and Schoeffer, he never signed his printed books.

In 1462, there was a warlike conflict in Mainz called the Mainz Diocesan Feud. Many people in the town were killed as the town was plundered and Gutenberg fled. Archbishop Adolp Von Nassau took over the rule of the diocese. Gutenberg settled in the city of Eltville and managed a small press that he didn't own. Von Nassau changed his mind and asked Gutenberg to come back to Mainz in 1465.

Typography workshop. Old metallic letters for printing with old book.

Von Nassau gave Gutenberg an official title of Gentleman of the Court and approved a monthly salary for him as well as allotments of grain and wine. Gutenberg passed away in 1468 AD at the age of 70. Sadly, his contributions were not known worldwide at the time of his death.

Gutenberg Museum
in Mainz, Germany.

BINDING

GUTENBERG'S LEGACY

lthough Gutenberg never became wealthy from his inventions or businesses, he changed the world. If it hadn't been for the printing press, many people would never have had the opportunity to own books of their own. If you love reading, the world becomes open to you, and it's as easy as opening the pages in a book.

Gutenberg would have been surprised to learn that his invention spread across Europe like wildfire. Printed books brought learning to a new level and soon almost everyone could afford to buy a book. It's estimated that in Gutenberg's day, there were less than 30,000 books in all of Europe.

Metal Letterpress Types.

itin just a few decades, the printing press spread to over a dozen European countries and more than two hundred towns and cities. By the year 1500, the printing businesses in Europe had printed more than 20 million books. From the years 1501 to 1600, the output of books increased by a factor of 10 and there were 200 million books in print.

Old metallic letters for printing.

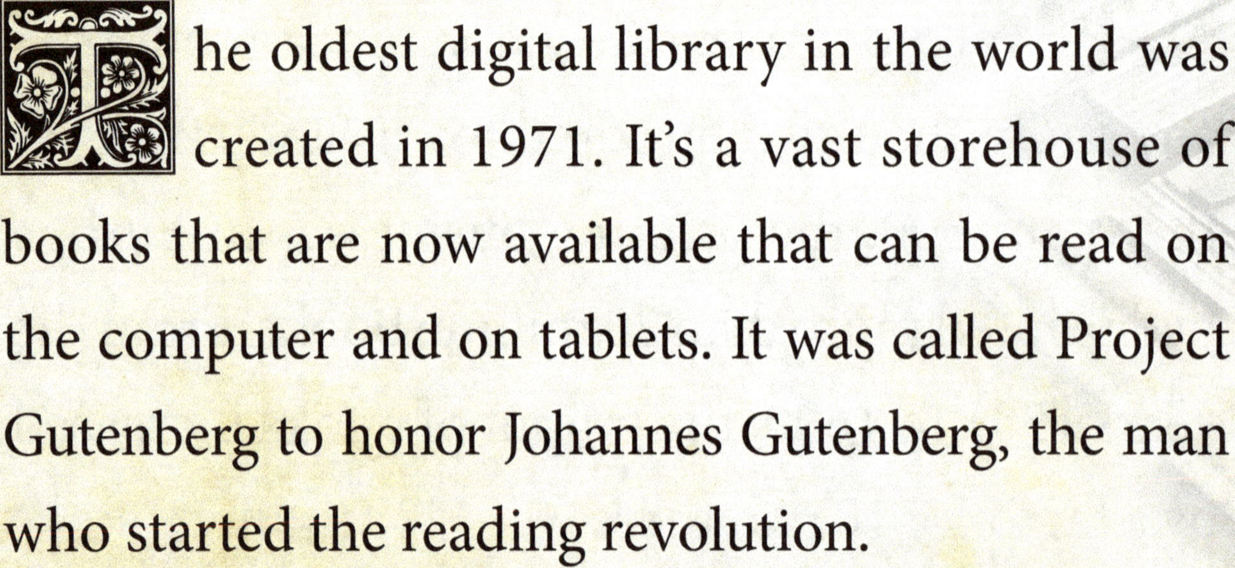

The oldest digital library in the world was created in 1971. It's a vast storehouse of books that are now available that can be read on the computer and on tablets. It was called Project Gutenberg to honor Johannes Gutenberg, the man who started the reading revolution.

Vienna, Austria: City landscape with Johannes Gutenberg memorial.

Awesome! Now you know more about Johannes Gutenberg and the legacy of his invention, the printing press. You can find more Biography books from Baby Professor by searching the website of your favorite book retailer.

Visit
BABY PROFESSOR
EDUCATION KIDS
www.BabyProfessorBooks.com
to download Free Baby Professor eBooks
and view our catalog of new and exciting
Children's Books